Introduction

Thank you for taking the time to pick up this book about Stoicism! Stoicism is an ancient school of philosophy, first developed around 300BCE.

In the following chapters, we will explore exactly how Stoicism came to be, some of the greatest Stoics in history, what the virtues and values of a Stoic are, and how Stoicism can enhance your life.

Despite being incredibly interesting as well as effective, Stoicism is not for everyone. Living the life of a Stoic often requires a lot of sacrifice, as well as discipline. As you will also discover, there is no such thing as a perfect Stoic. It is an ongoing daily effort to live life in line with the Stoic values and virtues, continually striving to become better.

Once again, thanks for choosing this book! I hope you enjoy learning about what it takes to live a Stoic life, and what exactly you can gain from embracing the Stoic way of living!

Chapter 1 - What is Stoicism?

Stoicism is a school of ancient Hellenistic philosophy that was developed by Zeno of Citium, around 300 BCE. It is considered as a refined philosophy of Cynicism that promotes the development of cardinal virtues as a way to overcome damaging emotions.

Today, being a stoic person is not reserved only for the followers of Stoicism. The word 'stoic' is now also used to refer to people who are known to endure hardship or pain without showing strong emotions.

However, Stoicism doesn't seek to completely eradicate emotions. Instead, it aims to explore specific virtues and to abstain from the pleasures of the world, enabling followers to develop freedom from suffering, inner peace, and clear judgment.

The Followers of Stoicism understand the reality that there are many things which we cannot control. This involves our earnings, our public image, and the opinions of other people. Certainly, there are ways to influence these things through our reactions and the way we respond, but predominately, these are things that are beyond our control.

Meanwhile, our own opinions, judgments, desires, and self-identity are the things that are within our control. It is interesting to take note that the things that we can control are all in the realms of our mind.

According to the essence of Stoicism, misery and suffering are mainly caused by the fact that people base their happiness on things that are ultimately beyond their control.

Modern Stoicism doesn't call for extreme detachment from all things that are beyond our control. Rather, things such as wealth, food, love, and sexual pleasures could be enjoyed by Stoics if there is a chance, but should not be actively pursued.

Basically, followers of Stoicism are not seeking pleasure from these things, and instead aim to still be happy even without them. Stoics can still live a life that is full of joy and peace, even without these worldly pleasures. However, if there is an opportunity to enjoy these things, Stoics can choose to indulge without guilt.

It is not easy to become a Stoic because the principles can at times be difficult to follow. In fact, Epictetus, a pillar of Stoicism, said that there has never been a perfect Stoic. He said: "I would love to meet a Stoic, but there is no one in full form."

The Stoic Sage is known as the perfect embodiment of the Stoic principles. Another pillar of Stoicism, Chrysippus, said that the Stoic Sage will be perfectly calm, even if you place him inside the Bull of Phalaris. This was a bronze bull, which was used by the cruel King Phalaris to torture his enemies. He would lock them inside of the bull, and light a fire underneath it, roasting them alive. As such, the Stoic Sage is considered as a divine being.

Physis: **Living in Accordance with Nature**

"Living in accordance with nature" or "physis" in Greek is the core principle of Stoicism. This principle doesn't refer to natural objects, or a state such as the natural color of the maple leaf. Rather, this term refers to the process that describes the way in which things are designed by nature to grow and change. Therefore, living in accordance with nature is to change and grow.

Of course, this fundamental principle is directed to humans, as there is no need to tell a rose to follow *physis*, because it is created to grow and change on its own. *Physis* is not also intended to tell us how to drink, eat, or breathe because these are all natural functions that are common to living things. With this core principle, Stoicism suggests living based on how human nature is designed to change and grow. But what really is human nature?

In the biological context, human beings have a specific genetic structure that has been developed, and is still going through the process of evolution. This process is governed by time and adaptation, and so nature is designing us to survive in our current setting.

Our level of success in this area depends on our circumstances (things that are beyond our control), and our choices (things we can control). While we have the genetic structure to develop a healthy body, our food choices could prevent us from achieving our potential. Even though it is only with our choices that we could align with nature, and in this case the food options that are healthy for us.

Physis, as the main motto of Stoicism, is the main message in the fifth letter of Seneca to Lucilius. But the early Stoic reiterated that it is actually not natural for us to eat food that is not tasty, as that could torture our great sense of taste. He was actually guiding early followers of Stoicism to align their choices with their physical needs. The principle of *physis* guides Stoics to seek for things that Nature has intended for humans to survive.

Nonetheless, Stoicism has survived in the modern world party because of this eco-ethical framing. Believers of stoicism view this as a guiding philosophy to take care of the natural world, which can be done through present-day endeavors such as reducing the carbon footprint, recycling, animal rights, and more. Modern Stoics are mainly aware of humanity's impact on the natural world - that we are totally part of nature and depend upon it for our survival.

In Stoicism, the context of human nature does not dwell on our behavior, but rather on our mindset. The concept of *physis* is to live while being mindful of our impact on our environment. But in a deeper sense, human nature refers to our natural design to grow and change in our efforts to reach our ultimate potential as human beings.

Stoicism and the Divine Being

Followers of Stoicism believe in one powerful and almighty Divine Being. While the fundamental values and principles in this philosophy don't actively encourage adherence to the Divine, it is assumed that worshipping a higher power can help an individual to easily embrace stoicism.

It is also interesting to take note that the Divine Being in Stoicism has no name, and also that nature in its wholeness is regarded as Divine. That is why many scholars of philosophy often compare Stoicism to Pantheism because the latter consider nature as a Divine Being.

In embracing Stoicism, you can better observe nature and experience how you can harness its power for your own growth. By meditating on the nature of the four basic natural elements - air, earth, fire, and water - we can better understand human nature. So regardless of your religion, as long as you believe that there is a Divine Being that governs our natural world, you can easily absorb the core values of Stoicism.

Stoicism has survived through history because this philosophy is founded on the pursuit of a life that is both satisfying and peaceful amidst difficulties and adversities. In fact, the stoic philosophy which was established in Ancient Greece inspired the formation and development of Cognitive Behavioral Therapy, which is a form of modern psychotherapy considered as one of the most effective ways to help individuals suffering from mental health issues.

The principles of Stoicism are mainly categorized into three parts - logic, physics, and ethics. Stoic followers believe that we can achieve happiness by pursuing virtues that can be harnessed by living in accordance with nature. In this context, Stoics believe it is crucial to understand the natural world so we can pursue happiness with ease.

Through mindful observation of the natural world, early Stoics concluded that nature shows a harmonious yet complicated setting, which is thought as the product of a Divine Being transcending the entirety of the universe. While Stoicism doesn't mention a specific name for this Divine Being, followers (with their own religious biases) often refer to this being as God, Zeus, Reason, Universe, or even the Mind.

Despite the religious context, it is important to understand that the concept of the Divine Being framed in Stoicism is not a supernatural being, but rather is something that is integrated with the fabric of the natural world. And as such, many Stoics consider Nature as the Divine Being itself.

With the wholeness of the Universe viewed as one great organism, of which we are a part, Stoics believe that past events could affect external events, and so the sequence of events is already established by fate. But despite this belief in predestination, Stoics do not advocate the perspective of being aloof with life. Instead, they promote the philosophy that is called "soft determinism". This is a concept that provides freedom despite a pre-determined existence.

This belief is rooted in the Stoic principle of human nature. While we have physical and mortal bodies like other animals, our existence is considered special because of our ability to reason. Our ability to think is seen as the manifestation of the Universe. According to the musings of Epictetus, many of us fail to recognize our inner divinity, which is our genuine self, and instead we develop an affinity to our mere mortal existence.

Through Stoicism, we can develop our inner divinity, thereby achieving an inner freedom that will not be affected despite the events in the predetermined Universe. Even though this freedom will not grant us the power to alter the course of our destiny, it will empower us to respond to events with active consciousness, and in the process take control of the impact of these events in our own journey towards pursuing happiness.

Stoicism and Religion

Stoicism as a religion is a common misconception among those who are new to this philosophy. While followers of Stoicism often make reference to the Divine Being, this is more philosophical rather than religious in nature.

Life after death is a common belief among major religions around the world. In comparison to this commonality, Stoicism is primarily concerned in how we live our mortal life. It doesn't guarantee a way to be saved from punishment because it provides us with a body of knowledge on how we can live amidst suffering.

With Stoicism, we can explore the particular aspects of life that are worth living, and develop a strategy for how we can achieve this level of being. This involves achieving tranquility or inner peace, which is the absence of negative emotions. In this quest to seek peace, Stoics are well versed with various psychological tools and strategies that you will later learn in this book.

Stoicism is not an established religion like Christianity, Islam, Hinduism, or Buddhism. However, it is still in harmony with these religions. For instance, this philosophy is quite compatible with the religious pursuit of trusting a higher power, as reflected in this prayer written by Reinhold Niebuhr:

> *"God, grant me the serenity to accept the things I cannot change,*
> *The courage to change the things I can,*
> *And wisdom to know the difference."*

This demonstrates a core belief in Stoicism that there are things that are simply beyond our control, and it makes more sense to simply focus on those things which we can control.

On the other hand, Stoicism is not a cult. You don't need to convert and practice certain rituals to be able to embrace and practice this philosophy.

There is no need to detest your material possessions, live in a cave, or shun your loved ones. There is no need to dress in white robes or sheepskin to be called a Stoic. But it is true that in understanding Stoicism and following its cardinal virtues, you may find yourself taking a closer look on your current way of living, which includes the way you dress, the way you handle your money, and the way you treat people around you.

Chapter 2 - The Most Famous Stoics in History

The founders of Stoicism are from diverse backgrounds. One was an emperor, another was a slave. One was a playwright, another was a water carrier. Some were wealthy, others were poor. Some were politicians in Ancient Greece, others were soldiers sent to battle.

But despite this variety, these people believed in the fundamental principles of Stoicism. Whether they were debating in the Roman Senate or serving their masters, they understood the essence of *physis,* and the power of focusing on the things that they could control.

In this Chapter, we will meet some of the most popular Stoics in history such as Marcus Aurelius, Seneca, Cato, Cleanthes, Epictetus, and Hecato. It is interesting to take note that these are only the Stoics that are known to us because they are mentioned in surviving historical evidence. These pioneers inspired a lot of people during their time, though there were surely hundreds of other brilliant Stoic minds whose legacies are unfortunately lost.

The Emperor

Perhaps the most popular Stoic leader in history is Marcus Aurelius, who was an emperor of the great Roman Empire. While he was born into a noble family, no one expected for him to rise as the leader of the strongest global force of the time.

There are limited accounts about his early years, but he was described as a serious young man who enjoyed hunting, boxing, and wrestling. Emperor Hadrian, the reigning leader when Marcus was a teenager, was childless. The old Emperor picked

Senator Antoninus (who was also childless) to take over the helm under one condition - he should adopt the young Marcus Aurelius. When Antonius died, Marcus was named as the new Emperor of the Roman Empire.

Marcus reigned for around two decades, from 161 until 180, and his regime was a tumultuous one – with the emergence of Christianity, the barbarian tribes attacking the northern part of the Empire, and the wars against the Parthian Empire.

Being a Roman Emperor was no easy task. It was considered the most powerful position in the ancient world. On the other hand, as an emperor, he has absolute power and absolute privileges. In effect, he could choose to indulge in worldly temptations, as he was answerable to no one. However, Marcus was considered a very wise and virtuous leader. He is among the Five Good Emperors of the Roman Empire who ruled with absolute power, but under the guidance of virtue and wisdom.

He is well associated with the development of Stoicism thanks to his diary known as Meditations, which are basically his private thoughts. In this diary, he often admonished himself to live a virtuous life.

The Politician

Seneca the Younger is one of the most popular Stoics in history. He was born more than two millennia ago in Southern Spain, but he received his education in Rome. His father is Seneca the Elder, who was a popular writer in Rome. He pursued a career in politics and also became a high-ranking clerk in the Empire.

In 41 A.D. Emperor Claudius banished Seneca to Corsica Island on the accusation of adultery with the emperor's niece. While on exile, he wrote letters to his mother to console her about his situation.

After eight years in exile, Seneca received permission to return to the empire through the efforts of Agrippina, who was the mother of future Roman emperor, Nero. In exchange for this favor, Seneca had to serve as the adviser and tutor of the future emperor.

Unlike Marcus Aurelius who was a wise and virtuous leader, Nero became one of the most tyrannical and notorious emperors of Rome. This raised questions about the true character and philosophy of Seneca.

Amidst the adversities that he had to endure, Seneca remained a stoic. He learned about Stoicism through Attalus, who was his teacher, and a Stoic philosopher. He also admired Cato, whom he regularly mentioned in his writings.

Even after his death, Seneca inspired other popular philosophers like Erasmus, Montaigne, Pascal, and Francis Bacon through his "Letters from a Stoic". This work offers timeless philosophical wisdom on life, religion, power, wealth, and grief. Below is an excerpt from the book:

"Believe me it is better to understand the balance sheet of one's own life than of the corn trade. We are not given a short life but we make it short, and we are not ill-supplied but wasteful of it. Think your way through difficulties: harsh conditions can be softened, restricted ones can be widened, and heavy ones can weigh less on those who know how to bear them."

The Soldier

Cato is another popular Stoic, and is considered as among the few philosophers who genuinely lived the Stoic virtues every day. Unlike Marcus Aurelius and Seneca, he doesn't have a written work that we can read today, but he is instead known for his actions.

He was first a soldier, and then became a senator. He was part of a noble family in Rome and was in fact known by the public as the Roman optimates' standard bearer. The optimates were the traditional group in the Ancient empire who regarded themselves as the guardian of the empire's constitution, and the defenders of the traditional government system that catapulted Rome from a settlement into a world empire.

History considers Cato as the most infuriating and most formidable enemy of Julius Caesar. He was seen as equal to Caesar when it comes to character, conviction, and eloquence. He could deliver a lengthy and inspiring speech before the Senate, and he was also capable of trekking the sands of North Africa on foot for 30 days.

George Washington, the first American president, regarded Cato as Liberty, because he was the last man standing when the great Empire was falling apart. Washington and his peers were exposed to the wisdom of Cato by studying the play written by Joseph Addison entitled "Cato: A Tragedy in Five Acts". Early American leaders would lift quotes from this play for their private correspondences and public speeches.

On the other hand, theologians and philosophers call Cato the Good Suicide, because of his persuasive and principled exception to the rule opposing self-slaughter.

Although an eloquent speaker, Cato was also criticized for his silence during important debates. His defense:

"I begin to speak only when I'm certain what I'll say isn't better left unsaid."

The Teacher

Among the early Stoics, Zeno has one of the most amazing accounts of how he discovered Stoicism. While seafaring from Phoenicia to Peiraeus, his ship was capsized along with his belongings.

Instead of despairing, he went to Athens, and there he visited a library where he discovered the musings of Socrates and Crates. The Athenian philosophers significantly changed his perspective, which resulted in him living by the principles of Stoicism.

Based on the account of Diogenes Laertius, Zeno said that he was now on a good journey after suffering from a shipwreck. In another account, he declared that Fortune had driven him to philosophy.

Zeno started talking about Stoicism at the Stoa Polkie - a prominent location in the Athenian Agora. In fact, the name of this location inspired the name of this philosophy. But of course, it wasn't immediately called Stoicism. Originally, the followers of Zeno were called Zenonians, but later were called Stoics as a nod to Stoa Polkie.

Certainly, the philosophy has developed a lot since Zeno first thought about his "fortunate" voyage. But still, the core message remains the same:

Happiness is a good flow of life, which can be achieved by gaining peace of mind. This comes from living a virtuous life in accordance with nature and reason.

The Slave

Unlike Marcus Aurelius and Seneca who were part of the noble families and the ruling class, Epictetus was born a slave. The diverse spectrum of Stoicism makes it powerful because it can provide timeless principles that are applicable to all, regardless of circumstance.

Epictetus was born around the same time as Marcus Aurelius and Seneca, in a place known as Hierapolis, which is now known as Pamukkale, in Turkey. He was the son of a slave serving in a noble household.

But his master, Epaphroditus, allowed the young Epictetus to study and with this, he discovered philosophy through Musonius Rufus who became his mentor. After the fall of Emperor Nero, Epictetus gained his freedom and was able to teach philosophy in Rome for about two decades. His career ended when Emperor Domitian banned philosophy in Rome. Epictetus fled to Greece where he established a school and taught there until he died of old age.

Epictetus is famous for many quotes associated with Stoicism such as:

"To make the best of what is in our power, and take the rest as it occurs." "Let death and exile, and all other things which appear terrible, be daily before your eyes, but death chiefly; and you will never entertain any abject thought, nor too eagerly covet anything."

Epictetus inspired Marcus Aurelius as well as other influential people throughout history. It is interesting to note that we only know the legacy of Epictetus thanks to a written account of his lessons through the notes of Arrian, one of his students.

The Water Carrier

Cleanthes was a student of Zeno, who followed his teacher's career and became the head of the Stoic school when the old master died. He was born in Assos, and during his teenage years he started attending the school established by Zeno.

According to the biography written by Diogenes Laertius, Cleanthes was originally a boxer who arrived in Athens with only several drachmae in his pockets. He first attended the lectures of Crates, before showing up at Zeno's Stoic school.

In order to support his pursuit of wisdom and philosophical studies by day, Cleanthes worked as a water carrier. During those days, it was unusual for regular folks, especially simple servants to study philosophy. Therefore, Cleanthes was summoned by the court in Athens to inquire how he could spend his whole day studying at a philosophical school.

Cleanthes was working during the night, so he was released by the court. In fact, the court was impressed by Cleanthes' passion that the judge even offered him a reward. However, the young philosopher declined as suggested by Zeno.

After the death of Zeno, Cleanthes became the head teacher, which was a post that he held for around three decades. Chrysippus, one of the brightest Stoic thinkers was a student of Cleanthes in Athens.

These men are only a few of the best Stoic philosophers throughout history. Other noted Stoic philosophers were Chrysippus, Gaius Musunious, Posidonius, and Panaetius.

As demonstrated in the diverse background of the pillars of Stoicism, it is evident that this philosophy is not reserved only for people who are from noble families. Regardless of your background and circumstances in life, Stoic principles can enlighten your path towards prosperity and happiness.

Chapter 3 - The Nature of Good and Evil

Stoicism does not encourage the avoidance of pleasure. Rather than classifying things as mere good or evil, this philosophy considers them as indifferent, and further categorizes them into preferred or dispreferred. One example of a preferred indifferent is wealth, while an example of a dispreferred indifferent is a blind eye.

There is no concept of good or evil in Stoicism, and it is not reasonable to be happy because you have a preferred thing (wealth) or be sad because you have a dispreferred thing (blind eye). Rather, Stoics are attaining to achieve the state of being happy, healthy and prosperous which is known as the state of *eudaimonia*. Stoics try to achieve this state by making the right decisions that are based on the cardinal virtues.

However, this doesn't mean that Stoicism denies the reality that we can experience pleasure from worldly means. For instance, we can certainly experience great pleasure from sexual stimulation or good food. In Stoicism, these things are acknowledged as preferred indifferent.

In Stoicism, you are free to pursue something and gain pleasure if you are consistent with your virtue. The pursuit of something should be avoided if you obtain it in a manner that is not consistent with the virtues of Stoicism. Remember, the toil will be temporary if you achieve pleasure through hard work. The pleasure will last longer. On the other hand, if you do something that is not virtuous just to get pleasure, the pleasure will be temporary and the dishonor could last longer.

For example, if you are stealing money just to buy luxurious items, the anxiety could still last even if the crime is left undetected, and the dishonor will haunt you if you are caught.

Guilt and regrets could remain, while the pleasure could vanish easily.

Stoicism and Death

In Stoicism, death is not avoided, as death is considered an integral part of the natural world. Many of us today detest the idea that we must die one day.

Avoiding the concept of death as well as thinking too much about our demise are two things that are not healthy. Death dwells in an area that we can't control. While we can do things to delay it, such as taking care of health and avoiding substances that could shorten our lifespan, there is no sure way to determine the exact date of our death.

Instead of being afraid or worried about death, Stoics regard it as a motivation for them to live in the present moment every day, and to eliminate all the negative emotions as much as possible. In Stoicism, you need to pursue simplicity in order to cut out your main source of stress. This philosophy is an opportunity to structure your life to maximize happiness and minimize drama.

If you live in the present, you can avoid being too worried about tomorrow. We can't predict the things that will happen in the future, so it makes no sense to worry about them.

Seneca's writings about death are considered to be comforting. He has a simple perspective on death – that we should focus only on the things we can control, and death is not one of them.

By adapting the Stoic view on death, we can resolve a common bad habit that we need to change today. Procrastination. We usually take time for granted because we think that there is always more time. Remember, there is no guarantee in life. So sort out your priorities and don't delay what you are planning to do.

The Stoic Duty and Virtues

Stoics are committed to their duty to make the world a better place. Aside from its concept of focusing on things that we can control, Stoics feel a social duty to help people become more aware of this themselves.

Stoics highly value work, particularly work that provides service to the society. It is ideal for people to look for a career that can fulfill his duty that provides a positive contribution to the society.

From the Stoic viewpoint, we can contribute to society by using our talents or resources for the common good. Are you an architect? Then design buildings that are durable enough to contribute to society's progress. Are you a teacher? Then educate people about the right principles.

Are you an entrepreneur? Then build a business that improves the people's quality of life and does not harm the environment. Are you a writer? Then write things that can inspire and motivate people to do good. Regardless of your career, you should make certain that your work will bring genuine value to society.

Don't worry if you have yet to discover your talent, or if you still need to start your own career. In fact, this is a good opportunity to embrace Stoicism as it may help you to start on a different path.

Remember, the essence of Stoicism is to live in accordance with human nature (*physis*). If you embrace this essence, you will understand that you have a duty to develop your talent in such a way that it can become a catalyst for change.

Meanwhile, our duties could change based on our natural relationship with people around us. According to Epictetus, our relationship with people must guide our own behavior, regardless of how they behave.

But in modern times, this argument can be difficult to follow. Should we honor our father just because he is our father, even if he is an alcoholic and does not provide for the family? Should we honor a teacher just because she is a teacher, even if she is not doing her job well?

Many of us would oppose this perspective. But it is important to keep your relationship in mind when you need to deal with the people around you. For example, your duty towards your own kin is different compared to your duty towards people you have just met. Your behavior could be different towards your supervisor at work than towards your college buddy. Hence, the nature of our relationship does, in fact, help in establishing our behavior towards people.

The core principles of Stoicism make it a distinct philosophy if you compare it to other philosophies of the Ancient world such as Cynicism and Epicureanism.

Stoicism and Christianity

Stoicism can be comparable to the philosophy that guided the foundation of early Christianity. In fact, it has been suggested that the ancient Hellenistic philosophy may have inspired the early Christians.

For instance, Saint Paul wrote letters to different nations in the Roman Empire as he took on the voyage after converting into the new faith. While travelling, he met different people with different practices, as well as philosophical convictions that have their roots in Greece. Therefore, it is not surprising that among the principles of early Christians was their desire to establish the foundation of the faith that was not purely intellectual, but also appealing to the people.

If we review Saint Paul's writings, we can discover key ideas that are arguably based on Stoic teaching. He could have encountered this philosophy while in Tarsus as he wrote in 1 Corinthians 11:14:

"Does not the very nature of things teach you that if a man has long hair, it is a disgrace to him?"

Stoic philosophy is also reflected in Saint Paul's perspective about putting faith in the Divine Being as part of our human nature, which is comparably aligned with Stoicism's theory of affinities.

Among the common grounds in Christianity and Stoicism is the concept of serving the will of the Divine. Neither Stoicism nor Christianity invokes the favors from God to follow our human bidding. This is in contrary to paganism, where rituals are practiced so the gods will follow human's desire. In Stoicism and Christianity, humans have the duty to follow the will of God, or the Divine.

It is also interesting to take note that Stoicism heralded the belief in one Divine, which was established by the teachings of Heraclitus in recognizing the one Logos. Eventually, early Christians would draw on the concept of Stoicism. And if we take a closer look, Stoicism is even more monotheistic if you compare it to Christianity, because it adheres to only one Higher Power. There are no opposing forces (the concept of good versus evil), No Trinity. No Saints. No Angels and Demons.

Meanwhile, searching for our purpose in life is another important concept for both Stoicism and Christianity. You may agree or disagree, but at some point, we are looking for a master to serve. This brings the philosophy popularized by Plato. If we make sex our master, then we will dance to the drum of lust. We will bend and twist in accordance with the nature of this god.

If money is your master, then you make yourself the slave of financial gain, and you might be tempted to do everything (including things that are considered illegal and immoral) just to make a profit.

In a sense, we are always looking for something or someone to serve, but some people are successful in abandoning the external masters so they can serve their inner divinity, or the Kingdom, as referred to in Christianity. In Stoicism, this self-servitude is not being selfish, but instead, it involves nurturing your growth so you can better serve the Divine.

While it may seem that Christianity adheres to the concept of the Logos in Stoicism, there is a significant distinction. Based on the musings of Saint John, Christ is the Logos made flesh. There is a major difference between recognizing a specific person in flesh and blood and recognizing an unknown force or providence.

In addition, the affinity of the Stoics to the Logos is also different with Christian affinity to God. The Stoic affinity is somewhat aristocratic - cold, distant, and intellectual. On the other hand, the Christian affinity to the Divine is Jewish in nature - argumentative, needy, and emotional. The Christian Logos thrives in love and praise.

The Christian eschatology is also more defined compared to Stoicism, although we have to consider the fact that the latter has been developed proactively over 2,000 years and has been solidified into dogma and doctrine. Christians believe that if you do good, you will be rewarded in heaven, but if you are a bad person, you go to hell.

In comparison, there is no such rewards-punishment system in Stoicism. There is no certainty of what will happen to us after we die. Stoicism is entirely a philosophy on how we can pursue happiness and prosperity in this world and not the afterlife. Meanwhile, Christians believe that we are already a fallen race, but we can seek redemption by accepting Jesus Christ as our savior.

On the other hand, Stoics believe that things will just flow, then will be destroyed by the Universe, and then the cycle begins again. These are interesting concepts, although the Stoic eschatology could be closer to astrophysics and more aligned with the Big Bang Theory.

It is also interesting to take note that many modern Stoics today don't believe in the Divine. They are simply non-believers or atheists. However, this doesn't mean that they cannot develop the rational agency to be live moral and virtuous lives. This fact makes Stoicism appealing to both believers and non-believers.

Chapter 4 - Stoic Logic

Another essence of Stoicism is to live a life based on logic, or reason. Stoics believe that the whole universe is governed by the Law of Reason. We can follow this law instead of running away from this divine force.

As a matter of fact, following the Law of Reason can be used as a strategy to achieve the essence of living in accordance with human nature. Nature has designed us to search for things that we need in order to live a meaningful life. The Universe also provides us with the opportunity to grow and change to reach our potential.

Our daily decisions can define if we really live in accordance with human nature through logic. Hence, the essence of *physis* is actually living a life that is based on virtues, because we are designed to be virtuous. We are naturally capable of following the cardinal virtues of Stoicism, but ultimately, we still have a choice to follow them or not.

In this sense, Stoicism will not help us achieve our aspirations in life. Instead, this philosophy will provide us with a systematic and philosophical way of living that will teach us how to achieve what we need, through virtue in the pursuit of prosperity.

It is important to take note that Stoicism is not a magical formula that you can follow to achieve the desired result. Instead, this is rooted from the inside. This guiding principle can be used to explore our own psyche, helping us to discover our misguided thoughts.

For most of us, this is a difficult task because it requires a significant paradigm shift. We must begin to see the unnatural identity of a life that is mainly directed by self-centered desires, actions, or thoughts for what it is from the perspective of Stoicism.

Stoic principles can provide us with some of the most relevant and practical sets of wisdom for living a meaningful life. In Stoicism, we focus on how we can become better human beings, and how we can live a prosperous life.

Achieving peace within through enduring adversity is one of the main goals of Stoicism. This can also be achieved by understanding the reality that our time is limited, practicing self-control, and being conscious of our impulses. It is crucial that we understand the challenges that we need to face, rather than escaping from them.

In the context of what we feel, it is not the external forces that are affecting our feelings, but rather, the thoughts in our mind. Once we understand that anxiety and stress are states within our own understanding and thoughts, we can become more capable of controlling the situation.

Instead of living a stressful life, we should understand that we are capable of controlling our response to anxiety and stress. There are times that we give in to anxiety, and in the process, we are giving it immense power by choosing to believe that we can't control our emotions. With Stoicism, we can control how we perceive these feelings and in the process, we can avoid the effects of stress and anxiety.

Stoic Logic and Fear

Franklin Delano Roosevelt was elected as the 32nd President of the United States during the time of the Great Depression. The people were afraid, the financial systems were in disarray, and the whole country was depressed.

During his inaugural speech, President Roosevelt inspired the whole country with his now famous quote "nothing to fear but fear itself." Part of his inaugural address reads:

> *"Let me assert my firm belief that the only thing we have to fear is fear itself - nameless, unreasoning, unjustified terror which paralyzes needed efforts to convert retreat into advance."*

It is basically illogical to be afraid of anything but fear itself. In fact, the things that we are afraid of are almost always worse in our mind, than in reality. Of course, an economic crisis is not a good situation, but panic will not change things.

The problems we face in life will not be resolved by being afraid, as it can only paralyze us from thinking about possible solutions. That is why it is important that we resist and reject fear if we want to live a prosperous life.

Gotta Catch Them All Attitude

Our modern society follows the principle of "Gotta Catch Them All". Many of us want to live a meaningful life while pursuing a high-paying career, establishing good family relationships, and experience worldly pleasures. But we should accept the reality that we can't have it all.

During the early years of Stoicism, the lecture hall in Ancient Greece was regarded as a place where people could contemplate the important things in life. They thought about their priorities and their relation to the external world.

Nowadays, we are usually too occupied with pursuing different projects or priorities that we ignore the importance of introspection. Instead of occupying our mind with various daily tasks, we can leverage the logic behind Stoicism by answering these questions:

- Can I live without it?
- What will be the outcome if I choose not to take action?
- Do I really need this?

Answering these questions will help you find inner peace, enable you to gain balance in your life, and get rid of the things that are not important.

Divine Logic from our Ancestors

One way to maximize learning in any endeavor is to find a great mentor. In Stoicism, you can look for people who have been practicing this Ancient wisdom, or read books written by popular Stoics.

The way we live and work should mirror the fundamental principles that we practice, rather than comparing, criticizing, and consuming. Instead, we should focus more on creating, learning, and living. Stoicism can help us better understand this ancient wisdom.

The logic behind Stoicism adheres to a life without suffering or passion. This is known as apatheia, which refers to a state of mind in which a person is not influenced by passion. Because of this, many people consider Stoicism as an indifferent philosophy. This notion is wrong because the pursuit of apatheia is not indifference, but rather an equanimity of the state of composure or inner calmness, especially amidst a difficult situation.

You should also take note that the concept of apatheia is different from the modern concept of apathy. In Stoic logic, apatheia refers to the quality embodied by the Stoic Sage.

Aristotle promoted the concept of living a virtuous life between excessive passion and deficiency. In contrast, Stoicism promotes freedom for all passions, while getting rid of our tendency to react emotionally or egotistically to any events in the external world.

Take note that we can't control things that are caused by Nature or by other people. We can only control our own will. But this doesn't mean total indifference from the world. Living a virtuous life could lead to satisfaction (eudaimonia) or to experiencing good feelings (eupatheia).

The logic behind Epicureanism and Stoicism are seen as opposing sides. Stoics believe that life should be virtuous and should be devoted to growth. Meanwhile, Epicureans believe that life should be spent in avoiding suffering, and instead, experiencing pleasure.

Nonetheless, both philosophies adhere to the notion that a vital part of a prosperous life (eudaimonia) was somewhat similar to tranquility (ataraxia), and living a life without passion (apatheia).

But there are major differences between the two philosophies, especially in the required perspectives and the way the ultimate goal in life could be achieved. Therefore, both apatheia and ataraxia are part of achieving a prosperous life, and even though the logic behind ataraxia is usually associated with Epicureans, both philosophies adhere to this concept.

In the context of Stoicism, it is important to remember that the term passion doesn't mean its modern meaning. Passion and emotion had a different meaning in the Ancient World. Hence, it is a huge blunder to regard Stoicism as a philosophy of living a life without passion.

Stoic logic categorizes passion into unhealthy and healthy groups. Unhealthy passions include fear, cravings, and pleasure, while healthy passions include discretion, will, and delight.

Stoicism and Epicureanism have a different logical approach when it comes to achieving ataraxia and apatheia. In Epicureanism, people can prevent pain or suffering by withdrawing from social and political life. It is ideal for Epicureans to establish close ties with people around them. Trying to play an important role in society is a sure way to have physical or mental pain, and so should be avoided.

On the other hand, Stoics accept their role in the society and try to work in accordance with human nature (growth) and fulfillment of their duty.

Chapter 5 - Stoic Exercises and Behaviors

By now, you should have a basic understanding of Stoicism, especially the concept of *physis* or living in accordance with nature, as well as the fundamental ideas behind Stoic logic and wisdom.

When it comes to physis, we are designed for change and growth. While the virtue of temperance (which you will later learn more about) is mostly about restraining from the tendency to be swayed by physical pleasures. Many of the exercises and techniques used by Stoics have significantly influenced modern psychological treatments such as cognitive behavioral therapy.

In this Chapter, we will explore the different exercises and behavioral techniques that are used by Stoics today. Many of these exercises have been developed through the years, and they are useful for anyone who wants to start embracing the principles of Stoicism.

Morning Reflection

Basically, morning reflection is thinking about how you would like to carry yourself throughout the day, and how you will approach challenges and obstacles that may arise. Below is a good example of a morning reflection written by Seneca.

Cling tooth and nail to the following rule: Not to give in to adversity, never to trust prosperity, and always to take full note of fortune's habit of behaving just as she pleases, treating her as if she were actually going to do everything it is in her power to do. Whatever you have been expecting for some time comes as less of a shock.—Seneca

Regardless of your religion, you must first try to express your gratitude to a higher power or the Universe that you are given another chance to live, as not everyone is presented with this privilege.

In your morning reflection, it is ideal to contemplate how you can embrace Stoic virtues and avoid vices. Select one particular virtue or strength that you would like to nurture, and think about how you want to integrate it into your daily routine. Try to think about how you would like to deal with any circumstance that you have to face for the day.

Then, you should instill in your mind that you can only control certain things such as your own thoughts and actions. Beyond this realm, everything is out of your control.

One advantage of being an early riser is that you can have a chance to go for a walk and take pleasure in the experience of breathing fresh air as you watch the rising sun. This is also a great opportunity to perform light exercises and start the day by taking care of your health.

One concept to think about is your own mortal existence, and the reality that your time is limited and your body will soon age.

The Stripping Exercise

The concept of the stripping exercise is that every situation is composed of various layers. Each layer could indicate something that we bring to that situation, and not the situation on its own.

In the stripping exercise, you should avoid thinking about your own image or any personal gain that you can take advantage of as a part of the exercise. Simply use it to contemplate a certain situation.

Basically, during this exercise you need to contemplate how you would like your life to be. You need to remove your ego from the equation, and ask yourself "what would the ideal version of me look like?" This should be thought about with regards to different situations and aspects in life, such as what you should do for work, or how you should spend your spare time.

It is crucial to think about the value of a particular situation. Moreover, you should also assess the types of qualities that a certain situation requires. You are fortunate if you have already developed the virtues that are important in Stoicism, but if not, then you may choose to regard the situation as a chance to harness these virtues.

Remember when we were kids and our parents or teachers would ask us what do we want to do when we grow up? Many of us said that we would like to be policemen, firefighters, lawyers, or doctors. Have you achieved your childhood dream?

Many adults today are in fact experiencing the so-called "mid-life crisis" because they are thinking about whether or not they are on the right track.

Through the stripping exercise, we can really explore what we want, such as finding work that is both fulfilling and meaningful. In performing this exercise, try asking yourself what you want to do if money is not an issue.

Stoic Journal

Writing in your own Stoic journal could be beneficial in your journey towards embracing this wonderful philosophy. However, writing in a Stoic journal is quite different than writing in a regular journal, because instead of writing only about the things that you have experienced, you will try to write your assessment of the circumstances that you will have to deal with, ideally through the Stoic lens.

As a philosophical tool, the Stoic journal can help you understand your own shortcomings and keep track of your changes and growth over time.

In keeping a Stoic journal, you can look back and check how your attitudes and behaviors have changed. This basic exercise is easy to accomplish with a regular daily journal, and when you do it properly, a regular entry will be no different than a Stoic one.

Before you start writing your Stoic journal, try first reading 'Meditations' written by Marcus Aurelius.

A View From Above

This Stoic exercise can remind us of our insignificance compared to the vastness of the Universe. This simple exercise can also help us to see a broader picture of any circumstance. In this technique, you need to use your imagination to attain a bigger perspective.

It is ideal to perform this exercise in a place that is quiet and where no one will disturb you. You can do this in your own room, but a park or a beach can also be a good place. You are free to use your imagination in this exercise, but it is best to start the view from above the clouds, and then slowly zoom into the ground.

Try to observe everything - cars stuck in traffic, the kids playing in the park, the natural landscapes, neighbors chatting, virtually everything that your imagination can reach. Be sure to observe and suspend your judgment.

Then, contemplate yourself and how you are associated with what you saw in your meditation. You should understand that many things that we think are important are usually relative. Hence, our importance can be relative.

There are different ways to perform this exercise. One way is through a time freeze, wherein you will imagine that the time has stopped and everything is frozen in time. Similarly, you can perform this exercise by thinking about a different era. With this, you will understand that there was a time that we did not exist in this world, and the day will come that we will also stop existing.

Negative Visualization

Negative visualization is a fundamental exercise in Stoicism, which will remind us how fortunate we are. This concept is quite easy to understand. In this exercise, you should imagine that bad things have happened in your life, and you have no control over these these negative things. You can imagine scenarios such as:

- Being childless
- Never having met your husband/wife
- Losing all your assets
- Losing your parents
- Getting fired at work

You must also think about how the situations that you need to deal with in the immediate future could go wrong. Some people think that negative visualization is a pessimistic approach, which goes against pursuing a satisfying and happy life. But if you think about it, this exercise can actually turn your life around, because you will realize that you are doing good in life, which is something you should be grateful for.

For example, if the car you are driving suddenly crashes and you die. What will happen to your family? Who will take care and support your kids? Through this exercise, you can prepare for the worst-case scenario.

Self-Control Technique

This Stoic exercise will enable you to experience physical hardships, and also help you to realize how you can live without the things that you are enjoying today. In a deeper sense, this can be considered as a practical application of negative visualization.

With physical self-control, you can prepare yourself in case you really have to go through physical difficulties or lose everything you have. You can also be able to train yourself not to yearn for things that are not within your control. Remember, you can only control your thoughts and actions.

In this Stoic exercise, you need to hold everything in life like it were loose sand. When you hold the sand tight, some will escape, but with balance and control, you are more capable of holding everything. One practical example of self-control involves avoiding sugary snacks or drinks or eating only within a certain calorie limit.

You should also remember that in this life, nothing is permanent. The people around us, the things we own, and even you, will one day perish from this world. Consider everything as temporary. Instead of saying that we have lost a loved one, you should consider it as giving him or her back to the Universe.

Musings of the Ideal Man

This Stoic exercise will empower us to contemplate the characteristics of the ideal man, specifically more on the psychological aspects, and less on the physical aspects.

What are the specific characteristics that make up the ideal man or woman? For some, this could be difficult to answer, and possibly, it is easier to focus on what an ideal man will do in any particular circumstance. According to the actions of this ideal person, we can try and determine their inner characteristics, and ideally begin to emulate them. However, we should make certain that we fully understand that the ideal man in this regard, does not actually exist.

Moreover, you can level up this exercise by making a list of actual role models and study what makes them worthy to emulate. Try looking for the best qualities of these people and set aside their negative traits.

Meanwhile, you can also contemplate the opposite of the ideal man. Consider the worst trait of humans, so you know exactly how to avoid becoming this person.

Self Retreat

Finding inner peace is a common reason why many people choose to travel. But while there are many advantages to visiting a new place, finding inner peace is not among them. Peace should come from within, which is something you can achieve without paying for a holiday trip. Visit a new place to meet new people, immerse in a different culture, and take pleasure. But if you want to find true peace, then you need to explore your inner world instead.

Self retreat is a Stoic exercise that you can do to explore the depths of your inner world. This simple exercise can be done anywhere and anytime. With this exercise, you can immerse yourself within your inner world, and find the freedom or peace of mind that you want to achieve. It is surprising that while humanity has already achieved amazing feats of exploration to understand the Universe or reach the deepest parts of the ocean, very few of us are able to navigate our inner world.

There is a lot more freedom in the inner world. We can be whatever we want to be. There is no need to visit a strange place just to "search for yourself". It will take at least five minutes a day to shut down your external world and explore your mind.

Are we really free? Or are we prisoners of our mind? People who love to read describe the experience as liberating. With reading, they can escape to any place and meet new people without leaving their room. On the other hand, the mind can become a prison cell. For example, people who are defeated by fear, anxiety, or depression are prisoners of their mind.

Stoic Philanthropy

In Stoicism, philanthropy is practiced as a way to promote the welfare of other people, and this is beyond making donations to different causes. Many of us would think that philanthropy is reserved for billionaires such as Bill Gates and Warren Buffet because they have a vast amount of resources. But Stoics believe that anyone can practice philanthropy by embracing the right attitude towards other people.

However, most of us tend to live as if we are imprisoned in a series of layers like a Matryoshka Doll, with each layer signifying a progressive distance from our true self.

How can we practice philanthropy as guided by Stoicism? As a Stoic, your duty is to bring more people into your circle. Therefore, you must consider your family and friends as an extension of yourself, and other people within your community as part of a bigger family. Next, consider all human beings as your own kin. With this practice, you will be more compassionate and sensitive to the needs of the people around you, even with strangers.

Certainly, a considerable shift in perspective is crucial in this practice, and it also takes a lot of effort from your end. With this mindset, you can acquire a larger circle of friends, helping you to understand different perspectives and backgrounds. However, you should avoid extreme attachment, because, like most things, relationships are also temporary.

Evening Reflection

Evening reflection, as the name suggests, is the counterpart of Morning Reflection. But in this exercise, instead of thinking about what will happen during the day, you need to contemplate on the actual turn of events. While you are resting on your bed, try to remember your day, and then try to answer these questions:

- Have I practiced the virtues of Stoicism today?

- What are the specific situations that happened today that provided me with the opportunity to nurture specific virtues?

- Was I friendly or considerate with the people around me today?

You can even write your answers in your Stoic Journal and try to assess the things that happened during the day, where you can learn valuable lessons. Also, try to include in your Stoic Journal specific things you want to change for tomorrow. With this Stoic exercise, you can recap your daily activities so you can better position yourself for change. The focus should always be on how you can be even better tomorrow, than you were today, even if only slightly!

Chapter 6 - Stoic Virtues

At this point, you must understand that following Stoicism requires living a life guided by virtues. In Stoicism, there are four cardinal virtues that followers should continuously practice and develop. The four cardinal virtues of Stoicism are the following:

1. Temperance
2. Courage
3. Justice
4. Wisdom

In this Chapter, we will briefly explore each cardinal virtue and provide practical insights that you can apply in real life settings.

Temperance

Temperance is the cardinal virtue of Stoicism that calls for self-reliance. This virtue will help you to limit your expectations about life, because too much expectation may lead to frustration, pain, and suffering. So rather than relying on others for your needs or happiness, it is best to depend on yourself and search for happiness within the inner world.

In the modern context, temperance is usually associated with abstaining from alcohol. In a sense, temperance can also mean staying away from bad habits. To pursue happiness, you should avoid things that can negatively affect your life. While this will depend on your moral compass, it is important that you embrace the virtues of Stoicism if you want to live by its principles.

The value of temperance can help you live according to the Stoic conviction. It is not just a habit of avoiding specific things in a list, but rather a fundamental positive purpose in this philosophy.

In understanding and practicing temperance, you can better realize the importance of properly using worldly pleasures such as money, sex, or food. Money can help you acquire the things you need to live such as a food, clothes, and home. Sex is crucial in procreation. And food, of course, is essential for our nourishment. With temperance, we can use these worldly pleasures in the right manner and for the right reasons.

How do you consume food? What about choosing meals based on their nutritional value and not for satisfying your cravings. Fast food chains in the US are popular for their huge servings as well as unlimited offerings. Bottomless soda, overflowing French fries, and large double burgers - are all too much to fulfill our biological needs. This is known as food intemperance, which is driven by our cravings and not nourishment, added with the commercial motive to encourage people to buy more.

Temperance can also be applied in your work. Through temperance, you can avoid spending too much time on your career that you begin to ignore your family duties. Many of us are working too much so we can buy a new car, a bigger house, or afford a world tour. Indeed, modern living has created this social and commercial pressure, which is only intensified through advertising.

Advertising, per se, is neither good or bad. It is just a mere technique to propagate information that can be valuable for the society. However, there is advertising content that could be detrimental to society. Companies use advertising to encourage people to buy more things that are not actually important to live a virtuous life. There is nothing wrong with advertising if the product can really improve your life. But if the contrary is true, advertising could damage our society.

But the popularity of advertising is something that we cannot control. Advertising is part of an industry that keeps the economy growing, which is arguably beneficial for society. Our response to advertising is something within our control, which you can do through Stoic introspection.

You should start by thinking about the things that you cannot resist. Are you eating too much fast food? Are you drinking too much wine? Are you weak against the sexual temptations outside of your marriage? Before you can develop the capacity to overcome these temptations, you should embrace the fact that you are weak, and that only through temperance can you live a virtuous life.

Courage

The decision to embrace Stoicism takes real courage because not everyone is capable of committing and fulfilling the required duties. But once you become more adept in this philosophy, you can experience the genuine satisfaction that you are contributing to a positive change in the world.

Courage is crucial in pursuing a career that is considered risky. For example, entrepreneurs are usually warned about the dangers of going into business, but still, they decide to follow a different path because they believe in their purpose. Similarly, artists also have to deal with the naysayers who usually talk about the financial struggles of the career, unless the artist becomes popular enough to sell their masterpieces at a lucrative price.

In general, many Stoics have to deal with the criticism brought about by a misconception of the Stoic philosophy. We are often considered as passionless and emotionless individuals as we try to avoid too much attachment with things that are only temporary.

In these situations, courage can help you to continue your journey. Aside from courage, you also need to develop your self-confidence. That is why you have to learn and understand the pillars of self-confidence. This will help you to develop the required courage in embracing Stoicism.

But before that, you should understand that self-confidence in the Stoic perspective is quite different. Self-confidence is not an idea or affirmation. In this philosophy, this is more of a practical application rather than a concept. Many of us are used to studying ideas comprehensively, sharing motivational words, or discussing ideas in a chit-chat. But in order to develop self-confidence, you should first practice confidence. In Stoicism, confidence is developed by the discipline of being constantly active in a specific manner.

It requires solid confidence to embrace Stoicism. Take note that self-confidence is not all about inspiring words or stimulating talks. This is more about living and practicing our purpose on a daily basis, with a focus on the six pillars of courage and confidence.

First Pillar of Courage - Personal Integrity

Integrity encompasses the ideals, conviction, standards, beliefs, and behaviors in Stoicism. If your behavior and conviction are well aligned with your virtues, you can easily demonstrate personal integrity.

Try to perform an introspection. Are your beliefs and behaviors congruent with each other? While this simple question can be answered by a simple yes or no, it may take some time before you can completely understand it.

In this pillar, it is crucial that you know yourself. Do you value honesty? Are you someone driven by success in the financial aspects of your life? Which areas are you capable enough to be successful? Which areas are your weak spots? Are you selfless or are you selfish?

The alignment of your beliefs and behaviors are crucial in measuring your personal integrity, which is considered as the main pillar of courage. Without personal integrity, you are not capable enough to avoid the temptations of the material world.

Second Pillar of Courage - Understand Your Life's Purpose

Understanding your life's purpose will significantly boost your self-confidence. Those who don't know their purpose are like old coconuts in the ocean. Just drifting and tossed by the waves. We can do better than this.

With Stoicism, we aim to understand our life's purpose, which will bring clarity to the things that are really important to us. When we are certain about our purpose, we can harness our inner divinity or inner power to align the goals that we want to achieve. These goals will motivate us to move forward through the invigoration of the body and the mind, and will bring more meaning to our existence in this world.

Are you now clear with your goals? What are the specific things that inspire you to rise up every day? It is ideal to write down your goals so they will be crystallized and aligned with your vision within the context of Stoicism.

Get a pen and paper, and then write down your ultimate goals in life. In the Stoic perspective, try to assess what you can contribute to making a dent in the Universe. It doesn't matter if it seems impossible at first. Just explore your mind to search for your vision. You can revise this later and convert it into a specific and doable action plan.

If you want to help people, what are the specific actions you should take? What do you have to do in order to build opportunities, help people, and grow as a person?

Third Pillar of Courage - Be Assertive

Being assertive is a manifestation of living a genuine life, because you behave and speak according to your authentic conviction and feelings. This follows Stoic living. The key concept of this pillar is to be authentic, which comes from the Latin word *augere*, meaning to promote, originate, or increase. Authentic shares this etymology with the word author. In the Stoic perspective, being authentic can be described as being the author of your own life story.

So you should try to ask yourself if you fulfilling the role as the author of your own life currently. Are you the one who is writing your life story or you are letting someone dictate the course of your life? Remember, the core concept of *physis* in Stoicism or living in accordance with human nature. We often have that intuition or gut feeling that seems to tell us if we are aligned with this conviction or not.

While there is no established scientific explanation behind gut feeling, it can be quite interesting to take a closer look into that force within us that can be bothersome if something is not right. This force will often tell us that we are not fulfilling our purpose.

For instance, we may feel bad because our career doesn't resonate with our core values. Or probably, you feel trapped in a relationship that doesn't bring value to your life. Some people yearn to travel, but don't because they are afraid of the financial constraints.

While there are specific things that you can do to prepare for these situations, you can still allow your gut feeling to rule. Once you embrace Stoicism, your core values will tell you if you are on the right track. Just be sure that you take action.

Fourth Pillar of Courage - Take Control of Your Life

You must bear in mind that you are responsible for your decisions and your actions. The context of responsibility in this sense doesn't mean accepting moral blame or guilt, but accepting your duty as the main causal agent of your life.

With Stoic courage, you can seek what you really love, pursue growth, and learn to be free. You can only do this if you are in control of your life. Despite your plans not happening as expected, your mind should have the courage to overcome any challenge.

Do you want to pursue a career as a visual artist, but your family doesn't want to support your dreams? Try to find a job first, and then hone your passion as a side project. The important thing is, you should not stop doing what makes you happy. If you consider Stoicism, you will understand that you don't have to source your happiness from people around you because you can always depend on yourself.

Do you want to start your own business but don't have enough financial resources? Try to pitch the business idea to venture capitalists or friends who can help you raise the money you need. There are also many types of businesses that require minimal capital.

Do you want to become a singer but you think your voice is not well refined? Many singers struggled early on their careers and had to undergo training before they broke through. Will you overcome this obstacle, or simply give up?

You need to be responsible for how you respond to the challenges of life as a self-reliant adult. Never give up, and never act as if you are a victim of an unfair society. Focus only on what you can control, and how you can improve things.

Fifth Pillar of Courage - Acceptance

Self-acceptance is crucial for seeking happiness. It can resolve our tendency for perfectionism, and it is a great element for the Negative Visualization that you have learned earlier.

This pillar involves embracing the fact that we are already complete and whole as we are, and no one is requiring us to be perfect. Nobody is perfect, so you should not think less of yourself if you don't have the "perfect" life. Embrace your imperfections and learn to love yourself.

The key is to find a balance between self-acceptance and your quest for growth. Remember the concept of physis - our nature as human beings is to grow and change. We must accept the fact that although we may not have the perfect body to be considered a supermodel, we still need to make sure that our bodies are healthy and fit.

Sixth Pillar of Courage - Living a Mindful Life

A powerful tool for practicing mindful living is through completing sentences. The basic idea of this exercise is to take the first part of a sentence and try to make at least six completions. Just be sure that every sentence ending is meaningful for you. Below are ideal sentences you can start with:

- If I focus more on my work, then...
- If I pay more attention to my wife, then...
- If I am mindful of the needs of the people around me, then...
- If I am more aware of my thoughts, then...

In Stoicism, confidence is developed by the discipline of being constantly active. You can't be a Stoic if you just declare one day that you are a Stoic. Instead, you need to be a daily Stoic who is courageous enough to endure the adversities that come with growth and change.

Justice

In the Stoic context, Justice refers to making the right decisions in life. It is important that as much as possible, our decisions are based on our conviction to live in accordance with nature. This requires a solid sense of morals before you can properly practice and deliver justice.

However, Stoics are not always required to deliver judgment, especially if the situation doesn't call for it. Basically, Stoicism also adheres to the concept of Karma, not in the religious context, but rather in the concept that we reap what we sow. And so, if we don't want to be judged wrongly and quickly, we should avoid the same. It is important for Stoics to be patient, and essentially you may choose to be indifferent in a certain situation.

In Stoicism, there is no requirement for you to help someone or to speak out. If you are not part of a situation, don't be involved unless you choose to do so, or if it is your duty.

One of the most appealing and powerful psychological tools of Stoicism is the acceptance of events that are happening, and acknowledging these many of the situations that we face are beyond our control. The primary reason that Stoicism is appealing to anyone regardless of their social background is that it can serve as a helping hand to cope with stress.

It is not surprising that Stoics are often seen as misaligned with the outer world or indifferent. The benefits of achieving inner peace come from the foundation of an inner fortitude that can place many Stoics in a delicate position, particularly in politics. There might be a misinterpretation in discussing the merits of apatheia. Some people think that Stoics are complacent or negligent, even there are social injustices happening.

In a broader perspective, many of the problems of the world are avoidable, especially if we can act together towards viable solutions. If Stoicism is encouraging passivity towards social injustices that are avoidable, or if Stoicism is promoting the act of blaming the victim for their own misfortunes, then is Stoicism not moral? This is simply not true. Stoics are mostly practicing the delay of judgment to further assess the situation and act based on their guiding principles.

Why Delay Judgment?

Many Stoics are in power - politicians, entrepreneurs, government officers, or high-ranking military leaders. Individuals who need to be calm and think amidst chaos can benefit a lot from Stoicism. Among the most important skills that leaders should learn is decisiveness. In crucial circumstances, it is important to take a step back and look at the big picture before making a decision.

But with the fast-changing world, people have to make more decisions in less time. Perhaps because of our desire to do more, many of us have developed the tendency to make quick decisions.

This is how Stoicism can help you in your career, mainly because this philosophy will help you to be calm amidst chaos, and to be more confident with your decisions. However, this doesn't mean jumping into quick assumptions before you understand a situation.

It is ideal to revisit every angle of a situation before you act. This is in fact among the many exciting areas of life. Even when we think we already understand something, you can often be surprised by learning more upon reviewing it once more.

In this sense, Stoicism calls for a delay in delivering judgment. With the rise of the information age, we now have the tendency to depend too much on using statistics as an alternative to using our guiding principles and virtues for judgment. While facts and figures are useful, our decisions should not only be based on data.

One important and valuable Stoic mind tool that you can use in making a decision is called silent contemplation. This is also known as mindfulness, or mindfulness meditation. After looking at all the data, asking people who are more knowledgeable than you for feedback, and looking at all the possible scenarios, you can take time to be quiet and simply think things through.

You can do this while taking a long walk, sitting in a quiet room, or even through a prayer. After this, you should act based on the data and the principles that are important to you.

Also, remember not to succumb to analysis paralysis. You must never delay unnecessarily, and you must find the right balance between contemplating and acting on your decision.

Wisdom

Embracing the Stoic philosophy requires doing the right thing. If we think it through, there are actually two types of decisions - the right choice and the easy choice. Take note that there is no such thing as a bad choice, because being "bad" is subjective. It might seem like a bad choice for other people, but it could be the best choice for you. Remember, it is always dependent on you, especially in areas that only you have control.

The followers of Stoicism always aim to do the right thing regardless of the consequences. Some are mild consequences, and others could be severe. Some Stoics even have to quit their means of entertainment such as gossip, mobile games, video games, and TV shows. Certainly, if you want to focus on your life's purpose, you need to make sacrifices. Changing the course of your life is not an easy task. This is the reason why Stoicism is not for everyone.

Stoic wisdom will provide you with the opportunity to become more resourceful, quick-witted, and develop good sense.

Being resourceful is crucial in the pursuit of happiness and prosperity. It is part of a Stoic mindset, and will help you a lot if the goals you have set are quite challenging or you don't have a clear vision of where you want to go. With Stoic resourcefulness, your mind will be more developed to always find a way or workaround.

The virtue of being wise and resourceful will inspire you to think outside of the box and visualize all the possible ways to achieve what you want, while still living a virtuous life.

By being resourceful, you are more capable of taking care of the problems that you have to face, and which are within your control. With Stoic courage and wisdom, you will be more competent in the pursuit of achieving your goals. This mindset is crucial in getting things done. This will develop in yourself your value, your work ethic, and your capacity to constantly follow through with your convictions.

It is crucial for Stoicism to hold the mindset that there are workable solutions for problems that are within our control. With Stoic wisdom, you can face any difficulties and be in a better position to overcome them.

Bear in mind that the Stoic virtues are integrated with each other, and each virtue reflects units. Developing one virtue is developing them all. The same courageous mind is also moderate, wise, and just.

Hence, the virtue of a Stoic is disposed of in a particular manner relevant to individual virtues. To help you remember the unity of the Stoic virtues, just consider that a person who is both a great orator, and a writer, and a doctor, is still just one person. Similarly, the virtues are also unified but are applicable to various areas of action.

Conclusion

Thanks again for choosing this book!

I hope you enjoyed learning about Stoicism, and are ready to begin embracing the Stoic way of life, through your virtues and daily habits.

If you enjoyed this book, please take the time to leave me a review on Amazon. I appreciate your honest feedback, and it really helps me to continue producing high quality books.